Muttaburrasaurus

Kimberley Jane Pryor

Marshall Cavendish
Benchmark
New York

Other Marshall Cavendish Offices:
Marshall Cavendish International (Asia) Private Limited, 1 New Industrial Road, Singapore 536196 • Marshall Cavendish International (Thailand) Co Ltd. 253 Asoke, 12th Flr, Sukhumvit 21 Road, Klongtoey Nua, Wattana, Bangkok 10110, Thailand • Marshall Cavendish (Malaysia) Sdn Bhd, Times Subang, Lot 46, Subang Hi-Tech Industrial Park, Batu Tiga, 40000 Shah Alam, Selangor Darul Ehsan, Malaysia

Marshall Cavendish is a trademark of Times Publishing Limited

Library of Congress Cataloging-in-Publication Data

Pryor, Kimberley Jane.
  Muttaburrasaurus / Kimberley Jane Pryor.
    p. cm. — (Discovering Dinosaurs)
  Summary: "Discusses the physical characteristics, time period, diet, and habitat of the Muttaburrasaurus" —Provided by publisher.
  Includes index.
  ISBN 978-1-60870-537-5
  1. Muttaburrasaurus—Juvenile literature. I. Title.
  QE862.O65P794 2012
  567.914—dc22
                                        2010037187

First published in 2011 by
MACMILLAN EDUCATION AUSTRALIA PTY LTD
15–19 Claremont Street, South Yarra 3141

Visit our website at www.macmillan.com.au or go directly to www.macmillanlibrary.com.au

Associated companies and representatives throughout the world.

Publisher: Carmel Heron
Commissioning Editor: Niki Horin
Managing Editor: Vanessa Lanaway
Editor: Laura Jeanne Gobal
Proofreader: Helena Newton
Designer: Kerri Wilson (cover and text)
Page Layout: Pier Vido and Domenic Lauricella
Photo Researcher: Brendan Gallagher
Illustrator: Melissa Webb
Production Controller: Vanessa Johnson

Printed in China

Acknowledgments
The author and publisher are grateful to the following for permission to reproduce copyright material:

Photographs courtesy of: National Science Foundation, Patrick Olmert, **9**; Photolibrary/© petpics/Alamy, **8**, **29**; Wikimedia Commons, Matt Martyniuk, **14**.

Background image of ripples on water © Shutterstock/ArchMan.

While every care has been taken to trace and acknowledge copyright, the publisher tenders their apologies for any accidental infringement where copyright has proved untraceable. They would be pleased to come to a suitable arrangement with the rightful owner in each case.

For Nick, Thomas, and Ashley

1 3 5 6 4 2

Contents

When a word is printed in **bold**, you can look up its meaning in the glossary on page 31.

What Are Dinosaurs?

Dinosaurs (*dy-no-soars*) were **reptiles** that lived millions of years ago. They were different from other reptiles because their legs were directly under their bodies instead of to their sides like today's reptiles. Dinosaurs walked or ran on land.

At one time, there were more than 1,000 different kinds of dinosaurs.

Dinosaurs lived during a period of time called the Mesozoic (*mes-ah-zoh-ik*) Era. The Mesozoic Era is divided into the Triassic (*try-ass-ik*), Jurassic, (*je-rass-ik*) and Cretaceous (*krah-tay-shahs*) periods.

This timeline shows the three different periods of the Mesozoic Era, when dinosaurs lived.

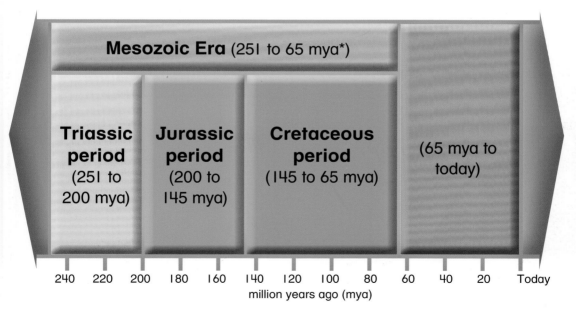

Mesozoic Era (251 to 65 mya*)

| **Triassic period** (251 to 200 mya) | **Jurassic period** (200 to 145 mya) | **Cretaceous period** (145 to 65 mya) | (65 mya to today) |

240 220 200 180 160 140 120 100 80 60 40 20 Today
million years ago (mya)

*Note: mya = million years ago

Dinosaur Groups

Dinosaurs are sorted into two main groups according to their hipbones. Some dinosaurs had hipbones like a lizard's. Other dinosaurs had hipbones like a bird's.

All dinosaurs were either lizard-hipped or bird-hipped.

Dinosaurs

Lizard-hipped dinosaurs

Bird-hipped dinosaurs

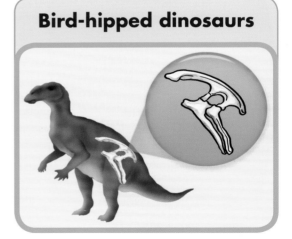

Dinosaurs can be sorted into five smaller groups. Some lizard-hipped dinosaurs walked on two legs and ate meat. Others walked on four legs and ate plants. All bird-hipped dinosaurs ate plants.

Main Group	Smaller Group	Features	Examples
Lizard-hipped	Theropoda (*ther-ah-poh-dah*)	• Small to large • Walked on two legs • Meat-eaters	Tyrannosaurus Velociraptor
	Sauropodomorpha (*soar-rop-ah-dah-mor-fah*)	• Huge • Walked on four legs • Plant-eaters	Diplodocus
Bird-hipped	Thyreophora (*theer-ee-off-or-ah*)	• Small to large • Walked on four legs • Plant-eaters	Ankylosaurus
	Ornithopoda (*or-ni-thop-oh-dah*)	• Small to large • Walked on two or four legs • Plant-eaters	Muttaburrasaurus
	Ceratopsia (*ser-ah-top-see-ah*)	• Small to large • Walked on two or four legs • Plant-eaters • Frilled and horned skulls	Protoceratops

This table shows how dinosaurs can be sorted according to their size, how they walked, and the food they ate.

How Do We Know about Dinosaurs?

We know about dinosaurs because people have found fossils. Fossils are the preserved remains of plants and animals that lived long ago. They include bones, teeth, footprints, and eggs.

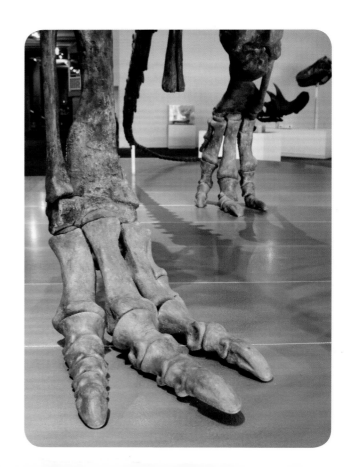

This fossil is the foot of a Muttaburrasaurus.

People who study fossils are called paleontologists (*pail-ee-on-tol-oh-jists*). They study fossils to learn about dinosaurs. They also remove dinosaur bones from rocks and rebuild **skeletons**.

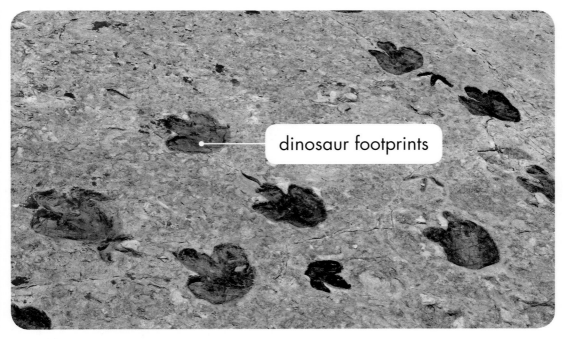

dinosaur footprints

Paleontologists sometimes discover dinosaur footprints, which are fossils too.

Meet Muttaburrasaurus

Muttaburrasaurus (*mut-ah-bur-ah-soar-us*) was a large, bird-hipped dinosaur. It belonged to a group of dinosaurs called ornithopoda. Dinosaurs in this group walked on two or four legs and ate plants.

Muttaburrasaurus was not a fierce-looking dinosaur.

Muttaburrasaurus lived in the early Cretaceous period, between 112 and 100 million years ago.

The purple area on this timeline shows when Muttaburrasaurus lived.

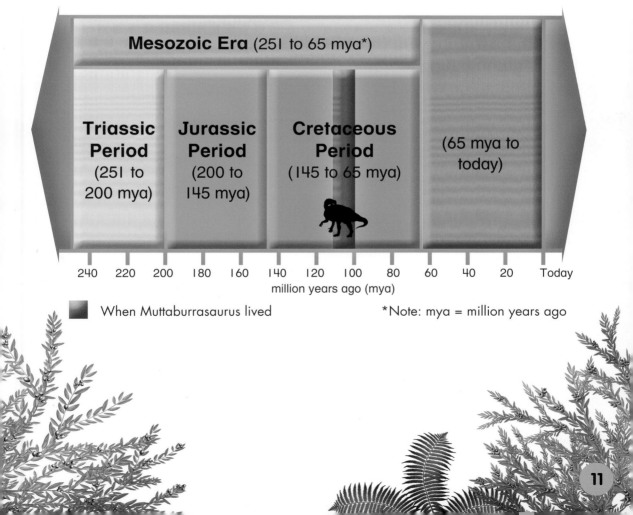

Mesozoic Era (251 to 65 mya*)

Triassic Period (251 to 200 mya)

Jurassic Period (200 to 145 mya)

Cretaceous Period (145 to 65 mya)

(65 mya to today)

240   220   200   180   160   140   120   100   80   60   40   20   Today

million years ago (mya)

When Muttaburrasaurus lived   *Note: mya = million years ago

What Did Muttaburrasaurus Look Like?

Muttaburrasaurus was 23 feet (7 meters) long and 7 feet (2 meters) tall at the hips. It weighed up to 4.4 tons (4 tonnes).

Muttaburrasaurus was as tall as an elephant and heavier than a hippopotamus!

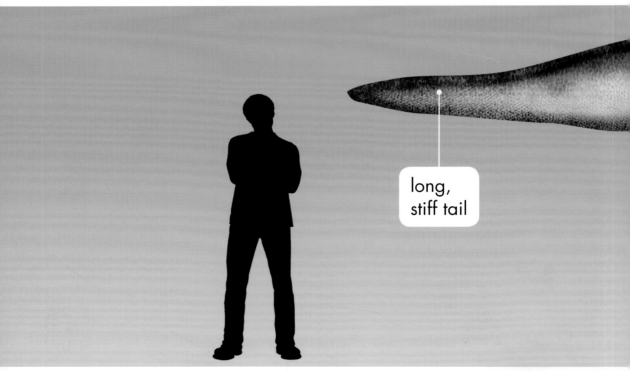

long, stiff tail

Muttaburrasaurus could walk on two or four legs.
It had a rounded snout, a muscular body, and a long,
stiff tail. It probably had scaly skin.

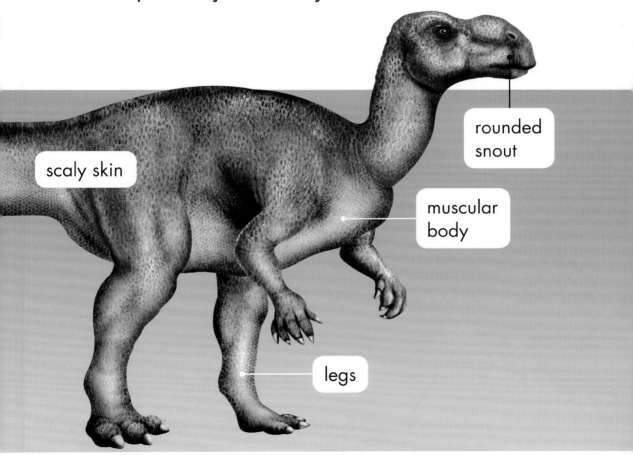

rounded
snout

scaly skin

muscular
body

legs

The Skull and Senses of Muttaburrasaurus

Muttaburrasaurus had an average-sized skull and brain. It may have been quite smart. Muttaburrasaurus had teeth in its cheeks that cut like scissors.

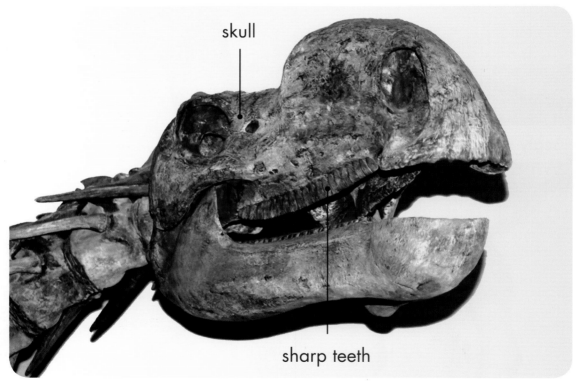

skull

sharp teeth

The back of the skull of Muttaburrasaurus was larger than that of similar dinosaurs.

Muttaburrasaurus could see its surroundings quite well. This is because its eyes were on the sides of its head. A hollow chamber on its snout may have improved its **sense** of smell.

The Senses of Muttaburrasaurus				
Sense	Very Good	Good	Fair	Unable to Say
Sight			✔	
Hearing				✔
Smell		✔		
Taste				✔
Touch				✔

Muttaburrasaurus Fossils

Muttaburrasaurus fossils have been found in Australia. This is the only place in the world where they have been found.

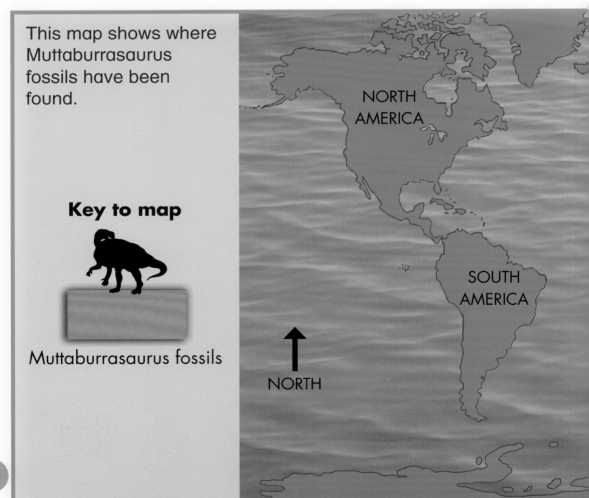

This map shows where Muttaburrasaurus fossils have been found.

Key to map

Muttaburrasaurus fossils

NORTH

NORTH AMERICA

SOUTH AMERICA

In 1963, farmer Doug Langdon found the first Muttaburrasaurus fossil. He found a skeleton near Muttaburra, in Queensland. A skull, bones, and teeth have been found since then.

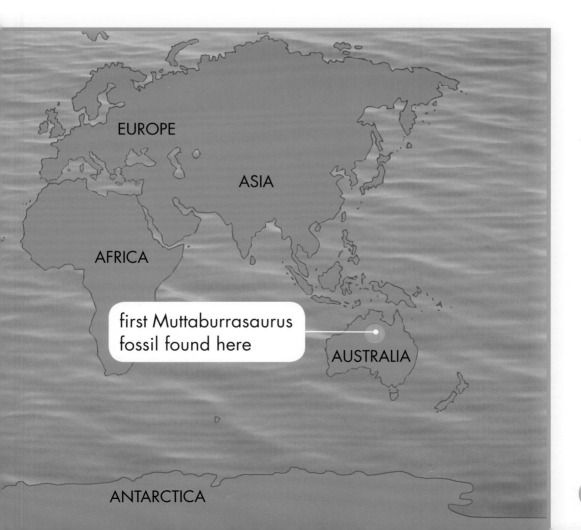

EUROPE

ASIA

AFRICA

first Muttaburrasaurus fossil found here

AUSTRALIA

ANTARCTICA

Where Did Muttaburrasaurus Live?

Muttaburrasaurus lived in conifer forests. These forests grew near a sea, in an area of Australia that is now a desert.

The conifer forests where Muttaburrasaurus lived had different kinds of plants, including cycads, ferns, and club moss.

Muttaburrasaurus lived in forests where it often rained.

ferns

conifer trees

cycads

club moss

What Did Muttaburrasaurus Eat?

Muttaburrasaurus was a herbivore, or plant-eater. It used its powerful, scissorlike teeth to eat tough plants.

Foods Eaten by Muttaburrasaurus	
Club Moss	
Conifers	
Cycads	
Ferns	

Muttaburrasaurus ate leaves that were up to 16 feet (5 meters) above the ground. It reached them by standing on its back legs.

Muttaburrasaurus could eat leaves that were too high for many other herbivores to reach.

Predator or Prey?

It is thought that Muttaburrasaurus was **prey** for large, meat-eating dinosaurs that hunted in conifer forests. Old, sick, or injured Muttaburrasauruses may have been caught, killed, and eaten by these **predators**.

An injured Muttaburrasaurus would have been attacked by predators.

Muttaburrasaurus protected itself from predators by living in a herd, or group. It warned the herd with a high-pitched call if it saw, heard, or smelled a predator.

Muttaburrasaurus protected its young by keeping them in the middle of the herd.

How Did Muttaburrasaurus Live?

Paleontologists think Muttaburrasaurus lived in a herd. This is because many large, plant-eating animals that we know today live in herds.

Muttaburrasaurus could have used the hollow chamber on its snout to call to its herd.

Some paleontologists think Muttaburrasaurus traveled south in the spring to find food and to **mate**.

Some paleontologists think Muttaburrasaurus traveled hundreds of miles each year.

Life Cycle of Muttaburrasaurus

Paleontologists study fossils and living animals to learn about the life cycle of Muttaburrasaurus.

1. An adult male Muttaburrasaurus displayed his rounded snout to attract a female. The male and female mated.

4. The baby Muttaburrasauruses joined a herd. They fed and traveled with the herd. They grew into adults.

They believe there were four main stages in the life cycle of Muttaburrasaurus. This is what it may have been like.

2. The female dug a hole in the ground and lined it with leaves. She laid ten to fifteen eggs in the nest, then covered the eggs with leaves.

3. Baby Muttaburrasauruses hatched from the eggs. For a while, their mothers brought them plants to eat.

What Happened to Muttaburrasaurus?

Muttaburrasaurus became **extinct** about 100 million years ago. Some paleontologists think it died out because of **climate change**. Climate change may have caused some types of plants to become extinct.

The food supply of Muttaburrasaurus would have run out if the plants it ate became extinct.

The last dinosaurs became extinct about 65 million years ago. Some paleontologists think climate change or volcanoes caused the dinosaurs' extinction. Many paleontologists think they died out when a large **meteorite** hit Earth.

Muttaburrasaurus could not survive changing conditions on Earth, leaving us with only fossils.

Names and Their Meanings

Dinosaurs are named by people who discover them or paleontologists who study them. A dinosaur may be named for its appearance or behavior. Its name may also honor a person or place.

Name	Meaning
Dinosaur	Terrible lizard—because people thought dinosaurs were powerful lizards
Ankylosaurus	Fused lizard—because many of its bones were joined together
Diplodocus	Double beam—because it had special bones in its tail
Muttaburrasaurus	Muttaburra lizard—because it was discovered near the town of Muttaburra, in Australia
Protoceratops	First horned face—because it was one of the early horned dinosaurs
Tyrannosaurus	Tyrant lizard—because it was a fearsome ruler of the land
Velociraptor	Speedy thief —because it ran quickly and ate meat

Glossary

climate change   Changes in the usual weather in a place.

extinct   No longer existing.

mate   Create offspring.

meteorite   A rock from space that has landed on Earth.

predators   Animals that hunt and kill other animals for food.

prey   An animal that is hunted and killed by other animals for food.

reptiles   Creeping or crawling animals that are covered with scales.

sense   A special ability that people and animals use to experience the world around them. Typically, those senses are sight, hearing, smell, taste, and touch.

skeletons   The bones inside the body of a person or an animal.

Index